THE

PROPHET'S

TIME

IN

RHYME

Part One

The Blessed Birth

.

Novid Shaid

ISBN-13: 978-0993044892

DEDICATION

To my parents and all the family

There is no God but Allah
Muhammad is the messenger of Allah

The Shahadah: The First Pillar of Islam

CONTENTS

Preface

The Prophet's Time In Rhyme is a tribute to the great and vast narrative poems that Muslims have composed in praise and remembrance of Prophet Muhammad, Allah bless him and grant him peace. Much of this literature is in Arabic and also in the ethnic languages of Muslims around the world.

The inspiration for *The Prophet's Time In Rhyme* is specifically from famous poems like Imam Al Busiri's, *Burda, the Poem of the Cloak* and also Imam Al Barzanji's mawlid, *The Jewelled Necklace* both of which possess international renown in the Muslim world. *The Prayers on the Prophet* were inspired by Imam Al Jazuli's blessed compilation: *Ad Dalaailul Khayraat, The Proofs of Goodness* which is also read throughout Muslim lands.

So, this book is a humble contribution to the genre of narrative poetry on the Prophet's life and prayers upon him. I hope that English-speaking peoples will appreciate this effort.

Finally, the collection of narrative poems at the back is a bonus feature which tell the stories of diverse characters both contemporary and ancient.

Peace and blessings upon our master, Muhammad, and his friends and family!

Novid Shaid, Rabbi Al, Awwal, 1436/January, 2015

The Prophet's Time

In Rhyme

Part One

The Blessed Birth

Prayers and Peace!
Most Perfect Peace!
Upon Muhammad
The Guide to Peace!
Bless his friends and noble line,
Listen to the rhyme
On the Prophet's time!

In a valley named Bakka
A building stood bare
A house made of stone
Once the centre of prayer
The first one to build it
Was the first ever man
Who dwelled in Heaven
His name was Adam
Who roamed and wept
In this barren land
After being cast down
Tricked by Shaytan
Allah Great and High
Told him and Hawa
To enjoy the garden
With its fruits and charms
But He gave a warning

To avoid a tree
Which to them was censured
By His strong decree
But the Shaytan slithered
And he whispered low
Hissing and coaxing
Take from its bough
So they took the fruit
And the Lord spoke clear
That they could no longer
Dwell in there.
Adam cried so deeply
To his treasured Lord
We have wronged ourselves
Mercy we implore
Adam and Hawa
To the earth were cast
On Mount Arafat
Reunited at last!
Adam built a house
In the valley so dry
A sacred house
Coolness of the eye
A house to summon
All the hearts and minds

To direct the souls
To the One Divine
So they lived and loved
Filled the earth with life
Their children spread
To other lands so bright.

Prayers and Peace!
Most Perfect Peace!
Upon Muhammad
The Guide to Peace!
Bless his friends and noble line,
Listen to the rhyme
On the Prophet's time!

But over the years and
The ages that grew
This house of worship
Was neglected and ruined
Until the arrival
Of a blessed seer
With his loving son
And his wife so dear.

I am a Prophet!

I am Ibrahim!
And I worship the God
Who fashioned the seas!
Who fashioned the sun!
And the moon and the sky!
Who causes the fire to burn and writhe!
Who causes the water to quench our thirst!
A blade to pierce and a bubble to burst!
My Lord inspired me
To find this place
To rebuild His house
For the human race.

So with his scion, Ismael
He laid each brick
With a spirit so real
When the final brick
Was fitted in place
Ibrahim and his son
Praised the Lord of Grace
Then he prayed to his God
For he was a visionary
And he raised his hands
To the skies so starry:

Oh Allah!
My Lord and Friend!
Who has no beginning!
Who has no end!
Send to the children
Of my children here
A special prophet
So wise and fair!
Who will teach them
The knowledge and
The wisdom so true
Who will guide them
Truly back to You!

Prayers and Peace!
Most Perfect Peace!
Upon Muhammad
The Guide to Peace!
Bless his friends and noble line
Listen to the rhyme
On the Prophet's time!

Allah
The Lord of the heavens and earth,
Answered his prayer

Such was Ibrahim's worth.
And so it transpired in 570,
When Bakka was now Makka
Crammed with deities
Where the Arabs bowed
To Uzza and Laat
Where the women were slaves
And poetry was art
Where the birth of daughters
Was divined a curse
Where the female babies
Were buried at birth
Where the house of God
Stood amongst totems
Where the love of wine
Was the town's custom
Where in that same year
Charged an elephant
Powerful and huge
On destruction bent
With an order to stomp
And crush the Kaaba
By the king of Yemen
Named Abraha
Where at that same time

Al Mutallib
Keeper of the House
From the House of Hashim
He petitioned God
To protect His house
From the charging horde
He was so devout
Where the army of Yemen
And their great elephant
Marched towards the Kaaba
With malevolence
Where a flock of birds
Were the saviours
Dropping lumps of clay
Upon the invaders
Falling to the earth
In a barrage and volleys
Raining on the soldiers
Pummelling their bodies
Where before the walls
Of the Kaaba so pure
The elephant froze
And advanced no more.

Prayers and Peace!

Most Perfect Peace!
Upon Muhammad
The Guide to Peace!
Bless his friends and noble line,
Listen to the rhyme
On the Prophet's time!

On that same year
A blessed lady dreamed
Of a light from her womb
And an angel unseen
Who proclaimed she would bear
A baby son
Who would guide mankind
His name: Ahmed.
Aminah she was
Daughter of Wahb
Wife of Abdullah
From Banu Zuhrah
And on that same year
When the baby arrived
His father Abdullah
Tragically died
The youngest one
Of eleven sons

Son of Muttalib
Noble and handsome.

Prayers and Peace!
Most Perfect Peace!
Upon Muhammad
The Guide to Peace!
Bless his friends and noble line,
Listen to the rhyme
On the Prophet's time!

So the baby arrived
On that same year
To his mother and kin
A deep source of cheer
Abdul Muttalib
Was suffused with joy
For Abdullah's child
For this baby boy
So he held the child
In his warm, strong hands
And encircled the Kaaba
In seven long rounds
Then he raised the child
And he praised the skies

He is Muhammad!
With a joyous cry!

Prayers and Peace!
Most Perfect Peace!
Upon Muhammad
The Guide to Peace!
Bless his friends and noble line
Listen to the rhyme
On the Prophet's time!

Wonders occurred
As the day elapsed
Signs and portents
With a great impact
The throne of
Persia's king collapsed
And the magian's fire
Fluttered and lapsed
And the Euphrates
Forgot its course
Comets lit the skies
Idols toppled with force
Allah, the Lord
And The Only One

Had sent a light
Brighter than the sun
He was Ahmed
Also, Muhammad
The final prophet
Of flesh and blood
That the Lord of All
The Beneficent
Sent to guide our hearts
To His Presence.

He was born to resist
Oppression and harm
To comfort the orphans
To revive and calm
To support the sick
And to feed the poor
To welcome any pauper
Knocking on his door
To honour the women
To reject idols
To restore the worship
Of the Provider
To reflect the light
Of The One Divine

To remind us
Of the Lord of Time
To impress the seal
On the one message
Carried by the prophets
In word and essence
To reveal the light
Which was fashioned before
All the worlds and time
With His love so pure.

Prayers and Peace!
Most Perfect Peace!
Upon Muhammad
The Guide to Peace!
Bless his friends and noble line
Listen to the rhyme
On the Prophet's time!

When the cries and the tears
Of the chosen one
Echoed in the air
Of the morning sun

The sun and the sky sent

Prayers and peace

And the sand and the seas sent
Prayers and peace

And the swaying trees sent
Prayers and peace

And the whirling winds sent
Prayers and peace

And the rocks and the stones sent
Prayers and peace

The birds and the fish sent
Prayers and peace

And the roving angels sent
Prayers and peace

And the roaming jinn sent
Prayers and peace

And the stars in the heavens sent
Prayers and peace

And the streaking comets sent
Prayers and peace

And the seven heavens sent
Prayers and peace

Jibreel and his host sent
Prayers and peace

And the Lord of the heavens
And the spinning earth
Who nurtures the world
And ignited its birth
Sent prayers and peace
On this blessed child
Whose light He fashioned
From the dawn of time
So join me now
Send prayers and peace
Upon Muhammad
The Guide to Peace!

Prayers and peace!
Most perfect peace!
Upon Muhammad

The Guide to Peace!

Bless his friends and noble line

Listen to rhyme on the Prophet's time!

Prayers On The Prophet

A Homage To Ad Dalaailul Khayraat

Oh Lord, send Your peace
and blessings ad infinitum,
Upon Our Master and
Liege Lord Muhammad,
whose face glows like the full moon,
whose smile dispels anguish and gloom
with locks like strands of silk
woven from a heavenly loom
with eyes penetrating, and radiating certitude
with perspiration of the rarest perfumes
with tears brimming with love and gratitude
the one who smiled in the face of ridicule
the one who endured
the curses of withering fools
the one whose face softened when he met
orphans, children, the poor and the bereft
the one who gave to those who withheld
the one who served others before himself
who stood in prayer until his ankles swelled
who implored his Lord, deep in the night,
while others slept
the final one to receive the Word through Jibril,
the only one who humbled the might of Azrael,
flag-bearer of Musa, Isa and Ibrahim
restorer of the light of Hajar and Ismail

and the moon split asunder at his behest,
and the sun turned back at his request,
and the spider's web and
the dove that built its nest
and the yearning palm tree and the Jinn
who were his guests
chosen above the whole universe
shown the face of God without hindrance
promoted above the multitude of mankind
the Prophets, the saints and the divines,
the supreme intercessor at the end of time,
humbled by the pure presence of his Lord,
sobered by the lights of Oneness of his Lord.
and his children, the diamonds of his heart,
the first to meet him in jannah, beloved Fatimah!
and his blessed parents, Abdullah and Aminah
and his cloak he spread for gentle Halimah
and his wives, sweethearts and counterparts
with the youth of Aisha and
the wisdom of Khadijah
and his companions of devotion
and humbled glance
in Badr, Uhud and Khandaq,
their faith enhanced
the Prophet, so longing for

the sweetness of Ramadan

for the taste of Zamzam and

the echoes of Quran

for the coolness of his eyes in dua

for the choruses of the angels from afar

the true servant of Ar Rahman!

the first and last love of Ar Rahman!

the splendour of Allah!

the wonder of Allah!

the gatekeeper of Allah!

the wayfarer of Allah!

navigator to Allah!

the liberator for Allah!

the final messenger of Allah!

the one who follows him

follows Allah,

the one who spurns him,

spurns Allah.

an nabi,

the priceless key!

the boundless sea!

the pinnacle of mercy!

the mirror of Divine decree!

the Arabian, uniting the tribes and

races of humanity!

Oh Allah, send your prayers
and unrelenting salaam
upon the Master of the Messengers,
the Seer of Islam,
and through this blessing, instil us
with patience and calm
and deliver us and our families from harm.
And finally we pray, Allah Almighty,
bless the spirit of our inspirer Al Jazuli,
for reciting his Dalail, make us worthy,
through it, bless us with health and security.

In the name of Allah
Most Gracious Most Kind
Verily Allah and His Holy Angels on high
Send prayers upon our Prophet,
most noble and divine
So invoke peace and blessings
which forever multiply
Oh you who truly believe in His signs.

Oh Allah!
Send Your prayers and peace upon him
And upon his companions and kin,
From the day You made this life

To the end when we arise
Every day a thousand times!

Oh Allah!
Send Your peace and prayers upon him
And upon his companions and kin,
By the number of
vowels that were ever pronounced
Whether they were
Explaining Your Acts
Entreating Your Peace
Inviting Your Delight
Invoking Your Power
Musing upon Your Truths
From the day You made this life
To the end when we arise
Every day a thousand times!

Oh Allah!
Send Your peace and prayers upon him
And upon his companions and kin,
By the number of letters
that were ever typed or written
In ever alphabet of every language
from the beginning

On palm leaves, leaves of paper and on rocks
On every screen, scroll, sign, tablet or box,
On every piece of cardboard, metal,
whatever size,
From the day You made this life
To the end when we arise
Every day a thousand times!

Oh Allah!
Send Your peace and prayers upon him
And upon his companions and kin
By the number of
people who ever walked and ate,
Of every racial hue, height, size and weight
Of every shape, figure, tribe and state
Of those densely crowded
in sprawling cityscapes
And those dotted sparsely
on country landscapes
From the day You made this life
To the end when we arise
Every day a thousand times!

Oh Allah!
Send Your peace and prayers upon him

And upon his companions and kin
By the number of
every living species and things
By the numbers of
fish gliding smoothly with their fins
By the number of
birds that flock the sky
And the swarming insects in regions wet and dry
From the day You made this life
To the end when we arise
Every day a thousand times!

Oh Allah!
Send Your peace and prayers upon him
And upon his companions and kin
By the numbers of
atoms fixed in our reality
Of every proton charging positively
And of every neutron, firing neutrally
By the number of
every charging unit of electricity
And of every weight of force
pulling magnetically
From the day You made this life
To the end when we arise

Every day a thousand times!

Oh Allah!
Send Your peace and prayers upon him
And upon his companions and kin
By the number of
tears shed by grieving lovers
And the hungry cries of babies
for their mothers
By the number of
embraces between brothers
In the number of
confiding words between sisters
And the smiles of rejoicing new fathers
In the number of
sweets offered by grandfathers
And the doting glances of grandmothers
From the day You made this life
To the end when we arise
Every day a thousand times!

Oh Allah!
Send Your peace and prayers upon him
And upon his companions and kin
By the number of

tears that Abu Bakr ever shed

By the number of

wise words Umar ever said

And the number of

coins Uthman ever spent

And the number of

shields Ali's sword ever shred

And the number of

children Khadijah bred

And the number of

narrations Aisha ever read

And the number of

wives the Prophet ever wed

And the number of

Nabi Muhammad's noble friends,

From the day You made this life,

To the end when we arise

Every day a thousand times!

Oh Allah!

Send Your peace and prayers upon him

And upon his companions and kin

By the number of

blessed steps Ibrahim ever took

By the number of

prayers Maryam ever invoked

By the number of

words with God Musa ever spoke

By the number of

sinners Isa ever purified

By the number of

Jinn Suleyman ever organised

By the number of

years Nuh lived before his passage way on high

By the number of

seconds, in the whale, Yunus spent inside

By the number of

children Adam and Hawa ever spread

And all the Prophets,

one hundred thousand!

From the day You made this life

To the end when we arise

Every day a thousand times!

Oh Allah!

Send Your peace and prayers upon him

And upon his companions and kin

By the number of

every verse of the Quran

Read with fear, love, hope

and to avert harm
By the number of
hadith which are bona fide
The true accounts of
Nabi Muhammad's blessed life
From the day You made this life
To the end when we arise
Every day a thousand times!

Oh Allah!
Send Your peace and prayers upon him
And upon his companions and kin
By the number of
every glorious sunrise in the east
And the number of
every haunting sunset in the west
By the number of
clouds that ever covered the sky
And the number of
stars that ever twinkled in the night sky
Of every drop of rain, snow or sleet
the sun ever dried.
From the day You made this life
To the end when we arise
Every day a thousand times!

Oh Allah!

Send Your peace and prayers upon him

And upon his companions and kin

By the number of salawaat that were ever sent

Upon Nabi Muhammad, the Leader of men,

By the number of

tawbah that were ever made

By weeping Momins

before the rise of day

By the number of

people who ever expressed

The pure shahadah

and felt nearness

By the number of

times our hands were ever raised

Asking for our needs

and hoping for Your Grace

By the number of

people who ever sinned

Then turned back to You

and made amends

By the number of

people who heard whispers from Shaytan

And averted his influence

by asking for Your safeguards

From the day You made this life
To the end when we arise
Every day a thousand times!

Oh Allah!
Send Your prayers and peace upon him
And upon his companions and kin
By the number of pearls of sweat on al buraq
Which cascaded as the sage ascended him
By the number of prayers the rider invoked
And the flutters of wings of his companions
By the number of sand stones at Al Aqsa
Which intoned his praise as he dismounted
By the number of Prophets that humbly stood
As the chosen one led with equilibrium
And the number of contours in the rock
And the streams of wind as the travellers took off
By the number of times the wise one was hailed
By each Prophet as the levels he scaled
And the number of shimmering branches on Al
Muntaha
Ad infinitum they communed Lover and Beloved
From the day You made this life
To the end when we arise
Every day a thousand times!

Oh Allah!

Send Your peace and prayers upon him

And upon his companions and kin

By the number of

times that You command "Kun"

And things come into being and fruition

By the number of

times You end life with death

And raise people in their graves

for their inquest

By the number of

times You make manifest

Your Divine Names

through Your actions and behests.

From the day You made this life

To the end when we arise

Every day a thousand times!

Oh Allah, send Your prayers

and unrelenting salaam

upon the Master of the Messengers,

the Seer of Islam,

and through this blessing,

instil us with patience and calm

and deliver us and our families from harm.

And finally we pray, Allah Almighty,

bless the spirit of our inspirer Al Jazuli,

for reciting his Dalail, make us worthy,

through it, bless us with health and security.

NARRATIVE POEMS

ON ISLAMIC THEMES

The Orphan's Song For The Kaaba

When I was fresh, new, suckling babe
My mother's poor spirit flew away
And my father died of a deep malaise
My life was shaping for a terrible fate
But by a stroke of eternal grace
I was taken in by a travelling maid
Nourished with her milk, settled by her face
I remember her clear soothing refrains:

Labbayk Labbayk!
Allahumma Labbayk!
Labbayk Labbayk!
Allahumma Labbayk!
Labbayk Labbayk!
Allahumma Labbayk!
La Ilaha Illalah!

As I grew in strength and the years ran by
I lived with my mother through some terrible times
Trekking through the deserts, perilous and dry
Begging in the cities just to get by
Slaving, watched by cunning, covetous eyes
Searching for a bed under the cold sky

And while we roamed, struggling to survive
Still my mother sang, tears filling her eyes:

Labbayk Labbayk!
Allahumma Labbayk!
Labbayk Labbayk!
Allahumma Labbayk!
Labbayk Labbayk!
Allahumma Labbayk!
La Ilaha Illalah!

Then my life caved in when I was a youth
When my mother one day revealed the truth
She had been like a solid, comforting roof
But now I was lonely orphan in sooth
She said, "*Listen my son, I made an oath*
To the Lord of the Kaaba and angels' hosts
That I would visit God's Almighty house
Where the whole of the world gathers round and round
So I was heading for Makkah nearly out of town
When I heard your shaking, adorable growl
Wriggling on the ground, wrapped in a towel
My heart wept to hear your miserable howl!
There I chose to raise you as my own little babe
Though I yearned to bow in the Kaaba's shade

Then I called on the Lord, don't abandon me!
All my wealth I will give to thee
I'll spend on this poor lonely baby,
But one day grant me the opportunity
To look upon Your House and sing with glee:

Labbayk Labbayk!
Allahumma Labbayk!
Labbayk Labbayk!
Allahumma Labbayk!
Labbayk Labbayk!
Allahumma Labbayk!
La Ilaha Illalah!

I wiped my tears and I kissed her feet
Saying: *"I will take you there on my own two feet!"*
Down the winding roads, through the heaving streets
Mother on my back, in the blinding heat
We pushed through the lands in gradual degrees
And hid in ships along the pounding seas
Never were we harmed by men or disease
As we said these words like a whispering breeze

Labbayk Labbayk!
Allahumma Labbayk!

Labbayk Labbayk!
Allahumma Labbayk!
Labbayk Labbayk!
Allahumma Labbayk!
La Ilaha Illalah!

After days and months, or even years!
Upon the horizon loomed Arabia
My poor old mother began to suffer
Our epic journey had exhausted her
But her eyes lit up with sheer wonder
"Take me my son to the Holy Kaaba!"
So we joined a group of dervish travellers
Pilgrims wrapped in white like glowing spectres
Reading tearful prayers to their Saviour
Treading down the path, chanting with fervour:

Labbayk Labbayk!
Allahumma Labbayk!
Labbayk Labbayk!
Allahumma Labbayk!
Labbayk Labbayk!
Allahumma Labbayk!
La Ilaha Illalah!

The road dragged on but we marched with cheer
Until we approached the epicentre of our prayer
Past the thronging mass of devotees
Swelling and flowing like a human sea!
Mother grabbed my shoulder with a grip so tight
Then she told me that she had lost her sight
"My dear own son, my orphan boy!
Wipe away your tears! You can't feel my joy!
I know my state doesn't make any sense
But alas life is a test of our patience,
My heart is filled with serenity
The lights of My Lord have set me free,
Though the Kaaba's veiled for me to see
Now instead I see the Lord is truly close to me,
But if you would like a smile to brighten my face,
Tell me what you see, describe the Kaaba's grace."

"Dear Mother it's like the Sun heating up all space
And the people, the planets, orbiting with haste
It's like the sky on a darkened night
And the pilgrim stars shining around it so bright
It's like a magnet that our Lord has fixed
And humanity crowds and encircles it
It's like the heart beating silently
And the blood flows around it eternally

It's like mighty Saturn, flattened into a cube
And the ring of pilgrims beautify the view.
It's the House of God, and He loves His guests,
And He answers all who make sincere requests,
How I wish dear mother, you could see it now,
For the sake of your honest, sincere vow."

Though her eyes were blind, she looked into me
Saying: *"My dear son, it is Allah's decree,*
My soul has drunk a cup which is forever filled
With the wine of love of our Lord's pure Will."
Her breaths gave up, she began to fade,
She would end her life in the Kaaba's shade,
But before my mother's spirit departed
She sang out those words, free and enchanted:

Labbayk Labbayk!
Allahumma Labbayk!
Labbayk Labbayk!
Allahumma Labbayk!
Labbayk Labbayk!
Allahumma Labbayk!
La Ilaha Illalah!

Notes

Labbayk Allahumma Labbayk La Ilaha Illalah- Arabic, Islamic prayers and formulas, meaning: I am at Your service, Oh Lord, There is no God but Allah.

These prayers are part of a longer prayer that Muslims say when they are embarking on the pilgrimage and wearing their ihrams, white sheets which signify purity, repentance and rebirth.

The Would-Be Salafi And The Would-Be Sufi

Once there were two neighbours
who were locked in a rivalry,
for one was a would-be Sufi
and the other a would-be Salafi.

"You're a man of shirk and innovation!"
argued the Salafi,
"You're an arrogant man," smiled the Sufi,
"You lack spirituality!"

"I yearn for past!" cried the Salafi,
"For the salaf us saliheen!"
"I yearn for the saints!" cried the Sufi,
"For the likes of Jilani!"

Whenever they passed on the pavement,
They would bicker like some angry bees!
"Where's your daleel for Milad?" roared the Salafi.
"Where's your ishq?" growled the pretentious Sufi.

"I'm the true follower of the Sunnah!"
"No! That title belongs to me!"
"You're not invited to my popular halaqa!"

"And we don't consort with ghair-muqallideen!"

It happened that one of their neighbours,
was a man of technology,
an eccentric, wild-haired scientist,
who had built a time machine.

So he thought he would conduct an experiment
To assess his time machine,
"I know, I'll try it on the Sufi!
And his friend, the Salafi!"

After putting the idea to the Salafi,
He said: "this sound likes a bida' to me!"
"Sound like you're a wuss!" laughed the Sufi
"Where's your faith in Allah's decree!"

"No one calls me a wuss!" said the Salafi
"with this experiment, I agree!"
"If he's doing it now," said the Sufi,
"Then it's definitely for me!"

So the scientists told them to listen
While he explained the intricacies,
"You have to explain your destination

Where'll you go for your first journey."

Then they both sat down in the contraption,
and strapped themselves in tightly
"To the time of Imam Ahmad Ibn Hanbal,
To Imam Hasan Al Basri."

And they bickered as the gadget travelled
Through time and the galaxies,
"Imam Ahmad is the true Salafi!"
"None can compare to Hasan Al Basri!"

With a thud and a great explosion
they landed far from the seas,
in the dominion of the stern leader
Mamun son of Harun Al Rashid.

When they emerged from their aircraft
It was too hard to believe
That they had travelled through time and the universe
To the time of the Salaf Us Saliheen!

And lo and behold who stood there
With a book in his hands, peaceful, at ease
But no other than the almighty scholar,

Imam Ahmad of the Hanbalis!

"Welcome my friends from the future!"
And the Salafi was on his knees,
"I'm not worthy of this my master!
You are the true Salafi!"

"But this isn't fair," said the Sufi,
"What about Hasan Al Basri?"
"Oh I'd loved to meet him," said Imam Ahmad
"Let's travel to him with speed."

So they took Imam Ahmad with them
Further on back in some degrees,
Landing on the shores of the Tigris
Where they found, Hasan Al Basri.

"How wonderful!" said the Sufi.
"You are the Imam of the pure Sufis!"
Then the Sufi and Salafi starting bickering,
Who was the truest in their beliefs.

But Imam Ahmad and Hasan Al Basri
Of the travellers they took no heed,
Instead they looked at each other

In a state of eternal peace.

"I am Ahmad Ibn Hanbal"
"I am Hasan Al Basri"
"You are the greatest of the Salafs"
"You are the imam of the pure Sufis".

"Let me learn from you my brother"
"No you're greater in mastery!"
"I love you for the sake of Allah"
"You remind me of the saaliheen".

Then in horror the travellers followed them
watching them speak so graciously
They loved each other like no other
This true Salafi and this true Sufi.

Suddenly, the travellers were excited
For the imams seemed to disagree
on a point of fiqh and aquida
it seemed they had different beliefs.

"Although we have our difference,"
"We'll agree to disagree,"
"But I still love you for the sake of Allah!"

"May He unite us again by the Lote tree!"

The would-be Sufi grumbled,
Frowning sat the would-be Salafi,
For their amazing journey had ended
Rather disappointingly.

After they gave their salutations
To Imam Ahmad and Hasan Al Basri
They asked the machine to return,
Back to the 21st century.

When the machine reappeared with a rumble
the scientist jumped up with glee,
"did it work!?" he asked with wonder.
"yes, it did," they both replied sadly.

And they went back to their houses,
shut the doors, this time rather quietly,
when they walked on to their different masaajid,
they avoided each other purposely.

From that day on something happened,
To the Salafi and Sufi,
Instead of bickering and fighting,

They offered salaams to each other rather meekly.

And they stopped labelling themselves with the titles
That they used before with such surety,
Because now they had learned the true meaning,
Of a true Salafi and a true Sufi.

When Terry And June Found Sukoon

Terry and June, the notorious two
scorned and reviled by their neighbours
husband and wife, walking trouble and strife
abhorred for their deplorable behaviour!

As they stumbled and screeched down the sanctimonious
street,
embroiled in a boiling domestic:
"You're a lousy liar! You're a rotten two-timer!"
"Stop whining you wench! You make me sick!"

Zayn and Bilquis, local Islamic activists,
would sneer at them, gawking from their bay windows
"They're the scum of the town, these Kuffar clowns!"
said the couple, with an air of haughtiness.

But Terry's nerves snapped and one day he cracked,
"That' s it you old cow, I've had enough!"
"I won't let you go!" Cawed June like a crow.
But Terry stormed out in a great rush.

Wherever he went, Terry would lament
Because behind him would follow a shadow

In rain, snow or shine, June would lurk behind
despite taking some harsh words and blows.

Feeling terribly cross, Terry strode past a mosque
Then an idea struck him like a bolt of lightning
"I know of a way, to keep June at bay
I'll pretend I've become a Muslim!"

With a skip and a jig, he entered the masjid
And June just stopped there and waited,
Then to her disbelief, Terry appeared on the street
Donning a white Muslim robe, which he knew she hated.

Not believing her eyes, June sank down and cried
While Terry pranced along back to their flat
Zayn and Bilquis screamed like a pair of banshees
"A Muslim now? Well, fancy that!"

Terry locked the door and leapt up with a roar
"I've finally got rid of that rot bag!"
But Terry's face dropped, when he heard a loud knock
And he opened the door to find June wearing a hijaab!

"I just don't care!" she declared with a glare,
"If you're Muslim or a bloody hari-krishna!

I'll do all it takes, to keep you in my wake
So you'd better get used to this Mister!"

In the following days, to Terry's dismay
June followed him to the masjid
But Terry thought that June would soon crack
She would never survive as a Muslim.

But something happened on the night of Al Qadr
As Terry was pretending to pray on his own
Inside the holy book, he was really taking a look
At his Facebook status on his IPhone.

Upstairs full of depression in the sisters' section
June felt hot tears streaming down her sunken cheeks
Despite her show of dedication for Terry's affections
He had hardly spoken to her in many weeks.

But June felt a shudder on this night of Al Qadr
For little did she know or perceive
That a troop of angels had around her gambolled
And prayed for her strength and inner peace.

At that blessed moment, June wept like a fountain
And her face, enlightened with heavenly beauty

A light shone in her heart, smashing her doubts apart
She accepted Islam with certainty.

Then she made for the exit, in a state of ecstasy
Feeling the lights of iman, intoxicating.
But just there before, she reached the masjid's doors
Terry happened to be there in conversation.

When he turned to her face and witnessed the divine grace
That Allah had bestowed on his erstwhile wife.
He was caught in her spell, a deep yearning befell
Him, he had never felt this way in all of his life.

Terry couldn't help, but to follow June's steps
Down the street and back to their flat
He caught up with her swiftly, looked at her gently
And said: "Allah has brought me back."

Arm in arm, joined by the hip, the couple walked up the
street,
In a state of unimaginable bliss
Eyes from curtains around, followed them as they walked
down
Uncomfortably, watched Zain and Bilquis.
From that day this couple, whose life once was struggle

Felt their hearts had finally become in-tuned

The angels rejoiced, at their sounds of their voices,

When Terry and June found sukoon.

Keep Coming This Way My Dear Friends!

When Naz and Beena, two drug addicts in love
one day repented, tears flowing like a flood,
that night they both dreamt of soft water flowing,
and heard a voice, far off, it said: "keep coming."

When Naz and Beena, well-known at the police station
fought their addictions, enlisting for rehabilitation,
that night they both dreamt of water smooth, with gentle waves,
and picked up that voice again, it said: "this way".

When Naz and Beena, the infamous lovers stained in heroin,
struggled against their demons, attending mosque sessions,
they saw water flowing, strange in colour, seeming not to end,
the voice much closer now, it said: "my friend."

When Naz and Beena, the ones the world had written off,
gained in knowledge, shed old skin, felt divine love,
the dreams kept coming, of water, more like milk,
but wholesome, fragrant and soft as the finest silk.

When Naz and Beena put their past behind them,

had a nikah, and strove to live like mo'mins,

that night they saw the Prophet, by the Hawd, beckoning them

Exclaiming: "Keep coming this way my dear friends!"

When The Goofy Gora Did A Roza In Ramadan

When this Goofy Gora did a roza once in Ramadan,
He fasted so well, he made us all feel real bad.
He took it so seriously that we thought he was mad,
this Goofy Gora who did a roza in Ramadan.

His name was John, a goofy, grinning, IT man,
said he was intrigued by Pakistan
by the people, their customs and their mysterious lands
so he said he'd do a roza in Ramadan.

We gave him some books to help him understand
And he said: "You're the best colleagues that I've ever had!"
He read all the books with such enthusiasm,
that now he knew more than us on Ramadan!

So he got up for sehri and ate some porridge and bran
learnt the dua for the roza like a Musalman.
He asked us about sehri, we struggled, to which he began:
"In the book it says sehri is sunnah in Ramadan."

Later in the office, working, starving and mad,
We mumbled and grumbled about our local imam,
But the Goofy Gora cried: "hey, listen lads!

No ghiba in your roza in Ramadan!"

During our lunch, we rushed out for the Zohr jamaat
down the local masjid, it was a little bit far.
Then while we were walking, the Gora stopped by in his car:
"I'll give you a lift; for the sake of Ramadan."

When the day had ended, the Goofy Gora looked sad
Coz we all decided to meet in a restaurant
To open our roza together as the likely lads
Forgetting to invite the Gora with his roza in Ramadan.

Later that night, we all dreamt of a terrible man,
With hooded cloak and mean like the guardians of Azkaban,
He stood like a giant, looking menacing and grand.
Then he thundered, giving us all a powerful command:

"Your Lord He loves your Goofy Gora who fasts in Ramadan,
And for the sake of him, He will not punish your manners so bad,
Take a lesson from him, look after your rozas in Ramadan,
He's the greatest friend that you could ever have!"

The next day at work, struck to silence and regretful calm,

one by one we asked one another about our dream of the
man,
when we realised the truth we dropped our heads feeling
damned.
coz there was no sign of the Goofy Gora who did a roza in
Ramadan.

When we asked our boss, he said, he didn't understand,
the gora phoned him late at night and said he was going
away real far,
He never came back, and we learned a lesson so hard,
To do our rozas like the Goofy Gora in Ramadan.

Until during one year, we all attended a biyaa'
One of the lads was getting married back in Pakistan
We all headed there quite sombre, now we were all like
mullahs,
But deep within we felt shame for the Gora and his roza in
Ramadan.

We got to the wedding in this village, in the pind of Punjab,
Where we saw something so crazy, we couldn't understand
For who was performing the nikah for this girl and our lad?
No other than the Goofy Gora who did a roza in Ramadan!

We watched him in shock, for this was completely bizarre!
He stood there reciting Arabic like he came from Arabia,
On his head a shining turban, and for dress, a kurta
The one and only Goofy Gora with the roza in Ramadan.

After the nikah, we approached him from afar
He recognised us, smiling broadly like we were long lost yaars
We all embraced and still couldn't believe he was the gora
That same Goofy Gora who did a roza in Ramadan.

"Thanks again!" he said,"for those books by Abdul Qadir of Jilan
I liked them so much, I travelled to study here in Pakistan,
I learnt so much knowledge here, that now they've made me Imam,
I've even learned the local dialect of the Punjab
Mei tossee ke faluda kelaasaa as now it's not Ramadan
And let's not dwell on the past but this is how it all began
You gave me some books, because I did a roza once in Ramadan!"

Notes:
gora: Urdu/Punjabi expression for white/English person
roza: Urdu word for fast, abstaining from food/water
sehri: Urdu word for pre-dawn meal before beginning the fast

biyaa: Northern Punjabi for wedding ceremony

pind: Northern Punjabi for village

kurta: long tunic worn traditionally by Asians in the Indo-Pak region.

yaars: friend in Urdu

Mei...kelaasa: Northern Punjabi, "I will buy you a faluda (sweetened milk drink/popular dessert in Pakistan")

Seven Nufus Were On The Loose

Seven nufus were on the loose
One day from Ramadan
They met in Sousse for some couscous
Before the maghrib azaan.

The first, a rioter, the sin-inciter,
The crazy imp, Ammara.
The second ilk, ridden with guilt,
Reproachful soul, Lowwaama.
The third, on fire, with love inspired
The stirring one, Mulhama.
The fourth, serene, like mountain streams,
The earnest, Mutmainna.
The fifth, contented, with perfume scented,
The honourable, Raadiyya.
The sixth, found-pleasing, the love unceasing,
The gracious one, Mardiyya.
The seventh, perfect, from the elect,
The wondrous, Kamila.

As they met and sat then began their chat,
Awaiting their great couscous,
Ammara cursed like the devil's nurse

His face twisted with disgust:

"This Ramadan; it does me harm,
I really can't be bothered!
One whole month, down in the dumps,
Pleasures are banned; O brother!"

"I'll try my best to pass this test,"
Lamented poor Lowwaama,
"I find it hard to stay on guard
I wish I was a llama!"

"I can not wait to taste a date
At the end of each day's fasting
A blessed time will here arrive,"
Mulhama said, forecasting.

"Enjoy the food, enjoy the mood,"
Exulted Mutmainna,
"Be pleased with fasting, grace everlasting
Purifying the sinner."

"I am contented with this unprecedented
Occurrence of Divine favour
Each year unique, with special mystique

I love Ramadan," Said Raadiyya.

"I am most pleased with His decrees,"
Celebrated Mardiyya,
"We are so blessed, with Ramadan our guest
It's sustenance from our Sharia."

"Come join me brothers! Let's rediscover
Our origins in Ramadan,
We're nothing but meanings, which is He conceiving,"
Said Kamila, so captivating and so calm.

"Don't give me drama!" argued Ammara
"I ain't missing out this month, mate!
X-Men will be on, the Euros are on
And a girl has asked me out on a date!
You keep up your fasting, I'll keep flabbergasting
the ladies with my exhilaration
I ain't got the time for things so sublime
Ramadan is a scourge on my reputation!"

Lowwama got haughty: "you are such a naughty!
Haven't you got any shame?
I don't find it easy; I find fasting queasy
But I'll still have a go all the same."

A smile had arrived upon the other five

Who sat eating their couscous so gently

"Ammara, we'll guide you, Lowwama we'll help you

Ramadan will fill you with plenty.

If you listen to us; follow without a fuss

Allah will make you His familiar

In just a brief moment, His works are so potent,

Ammara can become Kamila.

We are seven nufus, we're all on the loose

And our gathering here was intentional

The prince and the pauper, the sinner and scholar

Ramadan equalises our potential.

We are seven positions, in the Quran we are mentioned,

The seven degrees of the soul

Allah bless Al Shabrawi, wise as the Kalahari,

The author, the crown of the poles."

Notes:

This poem was influenced by the following work:

Degrees of the Soul by Shaykh Abdul Khaliq Al Shabrawi, translated by Dr Mostafa Al Badawi.

Nufus. Plural Noun, egos/selves/souls

And That's What Eid Means To Me

Down in the heart of Aylesbury
Lived a little bald man doing a PHD
On the mysteries of the Muslim creed
Like what on earth does Eid really mean?

Around he searched in the community
Interviewing a Muslim whoever he could see
And he told them about his mission to study
What on earth does Eid really mean?

So first he met a great grinning Mullah Maulvi
Who told him: "Truly Eid is from Allah's bounty!
It's a great celebration, a time to feast!
After we've fasted it's a great relief!
And that's what Eid means to me!"

Next came a grumbling, middle-aged auntie,
"Well, there's triple more cooking to do you see
From steaming chicken roast and gallons of mango lassie
When Eid is finished I'll put my feet up you see
And that's what Eid means to me!"

A little boy said: "I can't wait for Eid!

I get some wicked flashy clothes, and plenty of money!
I say, Eid Mubarak to my da da gee,
In the morning the mosque, with shalwar qameez
And that's what Eid means to me!"

"Yo, I chill it out with my bad boy hommies
We cruise on down with our beaming M3s
Filling the Broadway with our colours of green
Coz Eid is the time to show you Paki-stani
And that's what Eid means to me!"

A young woman laughed, "I really love Eid
I wear exquisite henna and gorgeous mehndi
I dress like a princess for all to see
All the colours they sparkle like a Christmas tree!
And that's what Eid means to me!"

"It's a very busy time, very busy indeed!"
Said the barber, "the rush you'll never believe
We don't get any sleep in the night before Eid,
Cutting and styling, getting them ready,
And that's what Eid means to me!"

"It's time for tremendous generosity!"
Said a lady, "feeding orphans and the poor needy

We think of others who may be suffering, we
remember those who aren't as lucky you see
That's what Eid means to me!"

"It depends who you talk to," said one of the momineen,
"It's a time for joy and humility
Uniting with your friends and your family
It's a day to remember Allah's limitless mercy
And that's what Eid means to me."

So off went the student with his PHD
He collated his notes and made a summary:
"it's all about food and looking pristine,
And enjoying yourself with your family
But it's for praising Allah really, ultimately,
Now I understand what Eid really means!"

Notes:
Da Da Gee: Urdu/Punjabi for paternal grandfather

The Dowdy Muslim

There once was a dowdy Muslim
whose face looked clumsy and cold.
She would waddle down the street,
looking down at her feet,
covered up in flowing dark folds.

When she trudged on through the markets
or stood in queue like a dull figurine,
the other women so dashing,
with bodies like mannequins,
considered her image obscene!

There once was a dowdy Muslim,
whom the men and women thought glum.
"If I looked so poor
I'd lock myself indoors!
She most definitely has no fun!"

This woman, she behaved so different,
wrapping her body, shying away from men.
When they peered at her dress,
they thought her oppressed:
"How old-fashioned! And so out of trend!"

There once was a dowdy Muslim,
whom the world around misunderstood.
While the people from her town
gave her disapproving frowns,
in secret she wished them nothing but good.

In the night when all were dozing,
she would rise and implore the skies.
Praying for security,
for her cruel community;
gentle tears flowing from her eyes.

There once was a dowdy Muslim
whose neighbour was particularly mean,
so offended and repulsed
by this Muslim's impulse
to obscure herself from being seen.

This neighbour was a proud professional,
an aerobics queen, with a facelift.
She went out with a doc,
who made a living from botox.
Who would lavish her with expensive gifts.

There once was a dowdy Muslim,

whose neighbour had a startling dream.

She witnessed her own fate

and awoke in a state,

letting off an ear-splitting scream!

This neighbour dreamed she was standing

on a plain with the rest of the world.

Feeling like a silly kid,

she stood there stark naked,

but none noticed or even said a word.

But as she stood and gazed around there,

someone caught her eye, standing so tall.

Beautiful as a pearl,

surrounded by whistling angels,

more delightful than a Princess at a ball.

Now the neighbour was extremely curious,

there was something so obvious and familiar.

So she left her place

from the rows of the human race;

the curiosity was nearly killing her.

When she reached this towering individual,

angels turned to her, so surprised.

They looked at her, up and down
giving her ridiculing frowns:
"Why ever have you left your line?"

"Excuse me, but do I know you?"
Gasped the neighbour, up to this glistening head.
When the figure turned its face,
the neighbour's heart raced
and her spirit was engulfed with dread.

For the figure was no other than the Muslim;
her neighbour, the sad, dowdy one.
Now she stood with such grace
pearls and jewels beautifying her face,
as if she were a chosen one.

"Where on earth am I?" shouted the neighbour.
"Why am I here, and how come you are suddenly so fine?!"
"Truth has conquered falsehood,"
said the Muslim as she stood,
"Inner beauty wins at the end of time."

Then the angels encircled and gambolled
with the Muslim, around and around.
Quick and gentle little sprites, weaving circles of light

Singing: "she's the best in town!"

"The best!" Woosh!! Woosh!!
"The best" Woosh!! Woosh!!
"The best in town!"
With a dance and a giggle
And waddle and wiggle,
The holy angels sang: "The best in town!!!"

So, there once was a dowdy Muslim,
whom her people cackled: "What a complete clown!"
But little did they know
of her deep, inner glow
as the hidden voices sang: "The best in town!!!"

"She's the best!" Woosh!! Woosh!!
"The best!" Woosh!! Woosh!!
"The best in town!"
With a dance and a giggle
And a waddle and a wiggle,
the holy angels sang: "The best in town!"

The Man Who Loved To Burn A Book

Once there was a man, who yearned to burn a book,
which millions loved; it was their special book,
its verses had some of them completely hooked;
they were delighted by just a momentary look.

But this man sneered; he confounded their desire,
to read this book, to follow and admire.
He thought it was wicked to even take a look
The proper thing he thought was to burn the book.

So he ordered many copies new and fine
Some people sent to him and some came from online.
He made a stockpile then everyday he cooked
A raging fire to sizzle all these books.

Suddenly his face appeared on every media
He even had an entry on Wikipedia!
There was great outcry; many labelled him a schnook!
For his intention to burn this special book.

When people heard, they ordered him to stop
His friends said, "Don't listen or you'll be a flop!
There's wickedness, there's violence if you look

The only thing to do is burn the book!"

Eventually the fateful day arrived
The bonfire ready and their faces full of pride
They gathered round inspecting every book
They couldn't wait to watch them being cooked.

They filmed them burning by the multitude
Films of it were uploaded on You Tube.
Frenzied people rioted, and their fists they shook
How dare this man abuse their special book!

But as the books were perishing in the fire
It sparked off many to search and to inquire.
What's all this fuss about? Let's take a look!
Why does this man love to burn this special book?

And every day this man prepared his fire
And giggled with his friends, watching those books expire,
More people couldn't help but take a look,
At the contents of this special burning book.

And finally when this man was feeling better
He was greeted with thousands of complimentary letters.
Some praised him for the work he undertook

But many thanked him for showing them the book.

Because now they read it every single day
They loved its poetry, and the message it conveyed.
And now they couldn't resist taking a look,
Because of the man who loved to burn the book.

The Little Girl Who Yearned To See The Prophet

"I want to see the prophet!"
Proclaimed a little girl,
"I want to look upon his face,
The mercy of the worlds."

"You've told me all the stories,"
She told her dear parents,
"But still I can not see his face
I'm feeling disenchanted!"

"Where did you get that word from?"
Replied the dad, impressed,
"I do not even use that word
Myself I must confess!"

"Oh daddy! When can I see him?
Oh mummy! Is there a film?
I'm starting to give up the hope
Was he actually real?"

The husband stared at his wife
Inside feeling the quakes
"I think we'd better get some help,
Let's take her to the shaykh!"
They led her to the masjid
And contemplating there sat
The shaykh in robes of pristine white
Crowned with a furry hat

"O Shaykh!" Complained the child
"This really is not fair!
Pictures abound of Jesus Christ
People can see him clear!"

The shaykh just sat there smiling
Replied with glowing eyes,
"There is a special way
That you can see him my dear child"

"A camera can not catch him
A pen can not impart
Seeing him is only done
With the eye of your true heart"

"First you need to love him
And his family
His blessed friends, companions
And his whole community."

"Then you need to picture him
By reading about his looks
If you ask your parents
They can read to you from books."

"His face outshone the full moon
His eyes intensely black
In them the light would dance and love
Expand and then contract."

"His hair was neither wavy
Or straight or tightly curled
His eye brows arched exquisitely
His nose perfectly curved."

"His mouth was wide and delicate
His front teeth slightly spaced
From his teeth a light would gleam
Enlightening the place."

"His face was slightly rounded
His hair fell to his shoulders,
His beard was dense, eye-lashes long
Delighting his beholders."

"When he walked it was as if
The earth rolled up for him
With pleasant voice and radiant face
He would meet the young and the aged."

"Between his two broad shoulders
Shone the seal of prophethood
When people met him just one time
They would love him for good."

"So read about his character
Picture him in your head
Then read upon him prayers and peace
And for him let the tears shed."

"When Allah sees in you the love
So serious and true
You'll see the blessed Prophet's face
Calling unto you."

So off the girl went home in wonder

Thinking about the Prophet

She asked the Lord with all her heart

And there she found the secret.

Raiders of the Lost Ramadan

"Quickly, Indiana!" Screamed his young sidekick
"Grab and bag that Ramadan
Before the beasts come quick!"

Indiana held his breath, outstretching his fingers
The kufi on his head slipping, sweat beginning to linger
That jewel, that priceless treasure stood
Tantalizing to his finger tips
Shining like an unearthly maid
Aromatic as a tulip
Gingerly, he took the jewel, in its place a sack of dust
Then he placed it in his satchel like a special trust
But as he retreated with a smile
He stopped for the ground shook
Short Round his loyal sidekick yelled:
"The beasts are off their hooks!"

Indiana seized Short Round and rushed along the passage
Behind them charged a savage beast, which roared:
"Come back and eat some cabbage!
Eat some meat! Eat some fish!
Eat like you're a monster!
Put that Ramadan back in place and drink some Coca Cola!"

They barely gave the beast the slip
Hiding behind a gigantic boulder
When suddenly they heard a voice
And looked over their shoulders.

"Come on boys, just follow me, toss that Ramadan aside,"
Whispered this ravishing goddess, a feast for their very eyes
Her eyes were so alluring; her voice as soft as silk
"Come with me and let me show you more of my ilk."
Indiana and Short Round turned away with great hardship
Suddenly, the goddess glared and shrieked: "right, that's it!"
In a flash, she transformed into a giant bat
Indiana looked at Shorty: "damn! We're in a trap!"

The bat swooped down towards them, red eyes and
gnashing fangs
Indiana leapt on a rope and swung like an orangutan
On and on they swung on ropes
The giant bat in pursuit
But now the two stood on the brink
Of a gaping hole in all these ruins.

"We have no choice," said Indiana, mournfully to Short
Round
And just as the bat came into sight

They stepped forward and tumbled down.

They fell at a furious speed

The darkness swallowing them

The hole awoke and spoke aloud: "ha! Ha! You are condemned!

As long as you hold this Ramadan so close to your heart

You will continue falling until your life just falls apart.

You can't handle all the change to your life and all the abstinence

You're falling in a great dark hole

Which was once filled with your lusts."

Indiana's face contorted into lamentation

But Short Round looked straight into him

"Be still, you'll get some orientation."

Lo and behold, with just that thought

Indiana felt like he was floating

No longer in an endless hole

But in the central masjid, standing

No longer was he Indiana

But a lad called Imitiaz

Short Round was just his little brother by the name of Shiraz.

After the prayer, they stayed to listen to a talk by the kaazi

His talk of fighting off the nafs made Imitiaz feel foolhardy

Looking at his brother he remarked: "the things that pass your mind in taraaweeh!"

Salman The Green Of Syria

Salman the Green of Syria
Roamed the streets in search of marifa
Missiles whizzed and whined above his head
Children hid and the skinny street dogs fled.
Salman the Green just stopped and observed the sky
The onlookers thought that he was one crazy guy.
Men with half their faces wrapped in red
Barked coldly: "Get down! Or you'll be dead!"
They hid and and reappeared in the crumbling alleys
Shouting again to him: "Look out! YAA HAAJI!"
Salman, the Green, looked to the air and then to them
And said: "I'm looking for what's beguiled all men!"
"You crazy fool!" They cursed: "Get off the street!
If one hits, you'll be nothing but burnt meat!"
Salman the Green, removed his emerald turban
And showed these men something, a terrible burden.
It was a ring made of burning rotten flesh
The men in red gasped with utter anguish.
"What the hell is that you crazy fool?"
They all yelled, disgusted and confused.
"It is the one and only ring of human desire
Which only can be shred in marifah's fire,
But I can not carry this ring anymore

Its weight is pushing me beyond the pure.

Shaytan composed this ring so he could wrap it round

The heart of every man in every town

Until the smell of lust had choked their brains

Until the taste of power flowed through their veins

And now they throw their fire from the sky

And women, children, families die.

The only way to end this spiral of hate

Is take this ring through marifa's gate

And let it incinerate in that raging fire

So let me be, while a search for something higher!"

Some moments passed, the men in red scarves stood

A missile struck a house, the ground nearby shook.

When they looked again, Salman the Green had disappeared

They didn't find his body as they had feared.

"What the hell was he talking about?" One of them remarked.

No one answered, but just for a while, some felt around their hearts.

The Living And The Dead

In honour of Sidi Ahmad Zarruq's maqam in Misrata.

"Knock it! Burn it! Pulverise it to the ground!"
They cheered uncovering Az Zarruq's mound.
"In the name of pure and unadulterated tawheed
We cleanse this wretched house of idolatry!
For Allah's deen this is a clear victory!
And may God curse those who make this dead man their
deity!
They barked and brayed as the saint's body was removed
A strange old man stood watching their jubilant mood
"What are you staring at old man, do you disapprove?"
Yelled one of the baying gang, derisive and rude.
"I'm staring at a mystifying sight."
Replied the strange old man, with eyes intensely bright.
"Oh yeh, old man, what seems to you so strange?"
"What's strange to me is that the ones whose hearts are dead
Are digging up such a one whose heart is truly alive
An idol, allegedly, has been obliterated
While the idols of your hearts have been exonerated.
But though you have this body, you can never touch his soul,
His soul is with his Lord, privy to all the secrets untold
And while you think you've rid the earth of a house of sin,

You've just sparked off a battle you can never win
Because you're not facing rows of swords or warrior jinn
It's not an emperor, it's the One and Only Him."

I Came Across An Atheist

I came across an atheist
who spoke with irony,
He asked me: "are you Muslim?"
I replied: "most certainly!"
He scoffed and cocked his eyebrow
regarding me with disdain
"how could you believe in" he said,
"a bunch of fairy tales!
That God, or is it Allah?
Made the heavens and the Earth
And He sent us all these prophets
Who were chosen at birth,
When now the body of science
Highlights what's true and false
You can't deny evolution
Chance is the way of course.
Your religion is just a reminder
Of how people used to think
To believe you must abandon
Your reason and intellect."
Well I just stood and listened
And this is all I could say:
"Well you follow your intellect

And I'll follow the spirit's way
You see where your reason takes you
I'll see where my spirit sails!"
"What a load of cobblers!"
He laughed in a great fit,
"It's all stimulated brain cells
There's no such thing as spirit!"
"Okay," I said, "Why don't you try it?"
"Okay," he said, "let's do.
I'll prove all this hocus-pocus stuff
Is totally untrue."
"Right," I said, "You have to
Submit yourself inside
Empty yourself of ego
Subdue your blatant pride
Then say these words sincerely
As if you believe it's right
When you say it with your tongue
Your spirit will take flight
It doesn't feel like brain cells
Buzzing all around
It feels like some eternal
Wind has left you utterly drowned."
"Okay," he laughed, "I'll do it,
"Just to prove to you

That spirit that you talk about
Is chemicals through and through."
So the atheist closed his eyes,
He closed off all his thoughts
Just to prove his experiment
Would prove all he'd been taught.
He whispered the shahada
He stood there very still
For a while he smiled somewhat
Then he shook as if with a chill.
He looked at me with wonder
But then with bitterness
"It's all in your head" he said
"It's all inside your head!"
But again he shivered
He tried to shrug it off
"That feeling is not from your heart
It's just inside your head!"
"Ah I said, you've done it
You've done it now my friend
Once you give your ruh some air
The yearning will never end."
"Ha, ha!" he said whilst trying
To veil his doubt with scorn
"This feeling is just cells inside

Don't you make me yawn!"
"But how did it feel?" I asked him
"When you emptied your inside
When you said the shahadah
And banished your great pride?"
His smirk suddenly vanished
He looked as if recollecting
Something that he so wanted to do
But doing it was forbidden.
He left without an answer
Proclaiming reason had won.
I chose to follow the spirit
To submit to the Only One.

When the Cynical CEO Saw the Treasures Of Lahore

For Data Saheb, Ali Al Hujwiri, Qaddus Allahu sirruhu

As he strode by blessed Bhatti gate,
The CEO's pulse quickened with contractions of hate,
for what he deemed a place of superstition and ignorance.
But his mother told him to pass by Daata's gate,
Weekly visits she instructed, to his growing distaste.
No longer just his mother's son, but a man of wealth and weight.
Earning millions, with a flourishing global trade.
Founder of his brand, with growing conglomerates.
Still his old mother insisted he pass by Daata's gate,
As he neared, he heard his mother's words reverberate
Entreating her son, so loving and affectionate
With these lines she had sung since he was a weeping babe:

"Mera Piyaara, Sona, Beita Gee
Allah give you tawfeeq
Mera Piyaara, Sona, Beita Gee
Listen to your mother's plea.
For success in your industry
Pray to Allah Paak with sincerity,
At the gate of our Daata Gee,

Allah will grant all that you seek,
Hidden treasure lies by Daata's feet,
For Allah loves our Daata Gee
He is with those of true poverty
See the gleaming luminosity
At the gates of our Daata Gee,
But most us we just don't see
This world has veiled us with its trickery,
The multitude's iman is weak
So have mercy with humanity
Listen Mera Piyara, Sona, Beita gee."

Mr CEO snarled at an urchin, eye-patched and thin
who approached, pleading for money, with an empty tin.
Cursing, confounding the dirtiness and scams
Beggars, drug pushers begging for money, what a sham!
What holiness could there by in such a place?
Full of mocking piety, blessings not a trace.
Frowning at a hag, bedizened with make-up and bells,
Next to Daata's entrance, with items, set up to sell.
Regarding the rickshaw men grabbing passengers
Hailing, hustling, hankering, circling like a flock of vultures.
Penetrating Daata's space, he glared with growing ire,
Instead of God, Daata was the people's only desire,
They had promoted some old man in Allah's place

All that talk of treasure and light by his mother was all fake,
Only darkness lingered for him, he had to disappear
Dismissing dua, he quickly escaped from there.
Later, remonstrating with callous colleagues from his firm,
Ridiculing Lahoris for the dead man for whom they yearned.
Shaking heads, while sipping on Mocas in their eatery
Feeling indignant of the excesses of their society.
When he reached his home, fuelled with determination
He kissed his old mum, then began his refutation:

"Meri Piyaree, Soni, Ammie Gee,
I've had enough of all this stupidity
For all this focus on your Daata Gee,
His gate has just become an absurdity
For people clutching onto backward tendencies
Your talk of treasure I just don't see,
Allah Paak is not their deity,
Meri Piyare, Soni Ammie Gee
No need for superstition or spirituality
Your hands and head can only give you victory!"
His mother's eyes glazed with sympathy,
And all she said with tears brimming inwardly:
"May Allah Paak show you what there is to see..."

The next morning Mr CEO rolled out with his shining Benz

Heeding hi s mother's wish he did not intend.
Cruising through the streets, towards his head office
Purposely avoiding roads which passed by Daata's presence
Suddenly, road blocks and accidents stood in the way,
Making him turn back, searching for routes, to his dismay.
But whichever way he chose the passage seemed closed
And the only alternative was to go by Daata's stronghold
With a heavy sigh, he drove on by Bhatti Gate,
Careful not to glance at what he deemed disarray,
Traffic slammed to a halt, and he heard a growing hum,
First merely a hint and then growing, like a coming flood.
Irritated, he emerged from his Merc
Checking, searching, seeking the cause of this disturbance,
Without realising, he was creeping back towards Data's space
Scanning the area he couldn't make out the humming's base,
Faltering, like the ground was shifting beneath his feet,
Perhaps he had caught some illness from the heat,
When suddenly, he backed into that old tramp on the road
Eye-patched, with money tin, on his back his life's load.
Eye caught eye, and suddenly without warning, time seemed
to stop,
Mr CEO's curtains between the truth suddenly dropped
To his horror he witnessed a sight that pushed him back,
Angels swarmed, flowing through every nook and crack,
Tiny, glowing like jugni, with the light of Allah,

Showering blessings made of gold coins into Data's Mazhar
Rubbing his eyes, shaken, the CEO questioned his head:
"Am I going mad?" He uttered, feeling growing dread.
Just then he noticed the eye-patched begging bum,
Now stood eight feet tall, magnificent, gazing down like a titan.
Cringing, Mr CEO gasped: *"What the hell is going on!"*
Around him, most people didn't notice, and just carried on.
Then caught his eye the bawdy hag he sneered at before,
Allah's light glistened freely from all the tacky jewels that she wore,
Something told him this woman gathered all the money she made,
Daily, distributing to the poor, while she fasted on most days.
Suddenly, the beeping horn of a rickshaw driver caught his ear,
Turning, he heard *Allah Hu!* Call out from the horn loud and clear,
This rickshaw driver smiling gave all his rides free of charge
To the poor and the destitute who came to join Daata's entourage.
Still the angels poured their treasures, while people walked by,
Unaware of what was transpiring in front of the CEO's eyes
He saw darkness exuding from people walking in and out

Of Daata's space, but light encircled it, squeezing darkness
out.
Some visitors and beggars' eyes brimmed with selfish desire
While others shone with the light of unity's loving fire.
Clutching his head, closing his eyes, hoping to clear,
From his brain, this crazy scene, this horrendous nightmare,
"What does this mean? Why don't people see!
Or is this just a figment, or a strange fancy!"
Then the giant tapped his shoulder, beckoning
the CEO to come forward so that he could whisper
something to him.
Stretching down, voice like a free wind, he said:
"The world has veiled us with its trickery, our hearts are
dead."

Then it was like the world slipped from under his feet,
He felt like he was poor man vulnerable and weak,
Collapsing on the pavement he began to weep,
The jugni angels swarmed around him like grazing sheep
Suddenly the resting place of Daata seemed to rouse from
sleep
And he heard the voice of Daata Sahab, pure and sweet,
Singing, *"Allahu Ahad, Allahu Daeem!*
Allahu Ahad, Allahu Daeem
Allahu Ahad, Allahu Daeem!"

Every coin that they angels threw, priceless and pristine,
Showered down like a fountain, one fell on him to keep
Tears brimmed as he examined this unearthly money
Inscribed with the words, *Allahu Ahad Allahu Daeem*
On the other side sparkling and extraordinary
"Muhammadur rasulullah khaatamannabiyyeen".
The CEO saw that Daata's voice singing: Allahu Daeem!
Formed a shield of light above, like a dazzling screen,
Cushioning the judgement that rained down from the
heavens
For many people who attended Daata's screen
Were riddled with ignorance and insecurities
But there stood some who were bathed in light, humble and
serene
For the sake of them and their Daata Gee,
Allah Paak held back the impact of His strong decrees
The judgments bounced off the light of Daata's screen
Like bubbles bouncing off and bursting immediately.
While the people strolled by, taking no heed
To the miraculous visions that the CEO had just seen.
he sobbed and wept draining himself of his own prestige
Crying: *"Why don't they understand, why don't they see?!"*
Then his old mother hobbled onto the scene,
With the priceless coins hanging around her body
As if she was an old, tremendous queen.

Holding her son's head close to her cheeks
Cradling and soothing him like he was a new-born baby
The CEO's mother sang her lullaby:

"Mera Piyaara, Sona, Beita Gee
Allah give you tawfeeq
Meri Piyaara, Sona, Beita Gee
There's no need to fear or weep,
You're safe here by our Daata Gee
Here in Daata's nagri
For most people they just don't see
They think their cleverness and surety
Is the cause of their victory
The world has fooled them with its trickery
For the secret of Daata's treasury
Is the purity of tawheed
And the Prophet's resounding finality
Allah bless him and praise him infinitely
Mera Piyaara Sona Beita Gee
Allah Paak has made you free,
Now thank him with all your energy
And honour those for whom He had decreed
His endless love and special intimacy
Like Nabi Paak and His Sahabi
And those of love like our Daata Gee,

Ignore the excesses you're bound to see
The people's ignorance is a disease
But Allah Paak is near in places like these,
If you would just look closer, if only.
Daata Ganj Baksh has a copious treasury
Not of gold, but the secret of tawhid,
Of Allah's Paak's absolute divinity
And his teachings are pure Muhammadi
Listen my piyaara sona beita gee."

Smiling, drowning in the sea of light
The CEO's mother held her weeping son, as the sun shone high
And Daata's space shifted and reflected the Divine kaleidoscope
True people visited, joining Daata Gee, clutching on to Allah's rope.

Notes:
Daata Saheb Ali Hujwiri: famous Sufi Saint and Patron Saint of Lahore in Pakistan
Daata Ganj Baksh: The Master who bestows treasures
Bhatti gate: gate near Daata Darbar- Daata Saab's tomb/mausoleum
"Mera Piyaara, Sona, Beita Gee"- My beloved, beautiful son (terms of endearment)
"Meri Piyaare Sone Ammie Gee"- My beloved beautiful mother
Daata Ki Nagri: The city of Daata

Allah Paak: Allah Pure of Imperfection

The Lover, the Birdsong of Baghdad and the Mythical Story of Inshaad

Once there lived a lover from Baghdad
Who loved God so much it nearly turned him mad
If he did not settle his nerves quite soon
He would disintegrate into a fiery pool.

So he roamed the Baghdad streets until nightfall
The fire of love burning stronger than a fireball
He had to find some respite from his illuminations
A channel for relieving and expressing his elation.

It just so happened that this lover had a voice
So loud and free it made all around him rejoice
But he needed inspiration, not being a trained singer
He yearned to sing for God with beautiful style and vigour.

His search went on, the yearning intolerably bad
When one dawn he noticed the birdsong of Baghdad
And at this moment Love inspired him with love
It was the moment he'd been dreaming of.

While sitting by the banks of the flowing Tigris
He sat among some trees as the sun was rising

Suddenly this lover's heart was tremendously lifted
Birdsong consumed the air, while along the Tigris drifted.

He saw a crested lark, migrating from Sheraz
Perched upon a branch singing with gravitas
The lover listened enrapt and spellbound
Imitating its melody he called it Nahawand.

Then singing for an absent friend or lover,
He heard a sighing Bul-Bul hailing from Basra
Its melancholic song echoed with the pain of separation
He called this one Saba and wept with trepidation.

A House Martin caught the lover's gaze thereafter
Singing about the haunting mystery of the holy Kaaba
He felt the fear of God, prostrating as
he listened to the bird, its song he called Hijaz.

Some cheer descended which made the lover glad
Some chirping blackbirds from the forests of Jilan
Their rousing song put the lover's heart at ease,
He called their song Bayat, Rasd and Ajami.

Then just before the lover ventured off
He heard a bird exulting in the glory of God

This swift from Nishapur, was on a journey, a true seeker
Inspired by its exultation he called its song Seeka.

And now with birdsong swirling round his head
The lover arose and saluted the birds of Baghdad
He sang their modes through days and through nights
And the people listened, imitating, lost in delight.

Notes:
Inshaad- the art of Arabic devotional singing
Nahawand, Saba, Hijaz, Bayat, Rasd, Ajami, Seeka- the seven modes of
music according to the ancient Arabic traditions. These modes are used in
reciting spiritual song throughout the Muslim world.

The Tragic Tale Of Tariq Azizee

Let me inform you of the story of Tariq Azizee
And the life of terrible cruelty he had to bear
Take heed of the tragic tale of Tariq Azizee
Let it balance your hope with some sobriety and fear.

For Tariq Azizee was a wonderful, energetic boy
Full of promise, quick thinking, humorous and young
But Tariq's father ruled him with an iron fist
Sneering, beating, restricting his freedom.

As he grew, Tariq felt stronger and wise,
His father's cruelty grew in intensity
Suppressing Tariq's movements and desires
His spies followed Tariq wherever he may be.

One day a throbbing desire filled Tariq's heart
He yearned for his own freedom and identity
So he crept and spoke to the people secretly
They heard his story, weeping with sympathy.

So a day arrived when Tariq stood before his father
Who brandished a whip, ready to punish some insolence
But when the lash came whizzing at his face

Tariq grabbed it with a look of sheer defiance

His father glared in horror as he turned and heard
Hundreds of angry voices breaking down the door
They streamed into the house, sweeping father away,
Who begged for mercy, as they took him, dragging him
along the floor.

Suddenly, Tariq broke down sobbing at the sight
Then smiled and laughed that now he was so free
The people cheered and lifted him on their shoulders
They had restored his life and dignity.

Then shortly after Tariq fell in love
Married a beautiful girl who bore him a son
And Tariq showered them with love and gifts
He lived the life he had always been dreaming of.

But as the years wore on and his son grew
Tariq found his fists raging on his wife and son
And though he hated himself, deep down he knew
That hidden deep inside, the tyrant still lived on.

The Meeting

Innamaa hadhihi hayaatu mataa' – verily this life is full of struggles-
Young Fata to Dhun Nun Al Misri– Kitab Ul Futuwwa
Abadan tahinnu ilaykumu arwah – forever do the spirits find rest with You
– Imam Shihaabudeen Suhwardi

When I was a restless youth
And my heart was searching for truth
A chance meeting transformed me
And I was born again, weeping like a baby.

It was as I roamed and strode
Through the streets, heaving in a state of overload
My head was grinding and saturated
With worldly worries and grasping faces.

And the world seemed dangerous and malicious
Talk and gazes looked so vicious
About the things that I believed
People burned my book of dreams.

Then I caught a glimpse of him
And I couldn't help but wince,
At the light which shone so bright
Right on through to a paradise.

He stood, helpless, back to the wall
surrounded by these menacing Neanderthals
who jostled, poked and sniggered,
laughing at his clumsy clothes and rough condition.

And though I was hesitant and afraid
These boys had cruelty written all over their gazes
I couldn't stop myself from saving
him, the lights pulled me in, amazing.

And when I stood before these guys,
without warning, they dematerialised.
And now I stood before his eyes.
I drowned in a sea of light, and cried.

He stood silent for a while
Handing me a cloth for my tears to dry.
Then he looked deep in my eyes
And sang to me these unforgettable lines:

"I'm a poor man on the road
I live without abode
Only scraps are good enough for me
Few desire to speak with me.

But when Your sun rose in my life
And Your moon reflects Your light
The warmth eases my pain
And pure cheer graces my days.

And when I meet Your special friends
Oh the joy and hope they bring
As we sing about Your light
While this aging world staggers by.

So take the rough and tumble on the chin
Fear not of people and their din
For this life is hope and fear,
The pain rides with the cheer."

Then he left and I never saw him again
But the anguish was cleared from my head.
And I saw things as they are
Lights engulfed me, spectacular.

Now I roam on through this life
With energetic children and busy wife.
Leaning on each other for motivation
Sometimes suffering the trials and tribulations.

But every now and then, we cry,
With tears of joy and heavy sighs
The lights of heaven shine and glisten
And I can't help but stop and sing:

"I'm a poor man on the road
I live without abode
Only scraps are good enough for me
Few desire to speak with me.

But when Your sun rose in my life
And Your moon reflects Your light
The warmth eases my pain
And pure cheer graces my days.

And when I meet Your special friends
Oh the joy and hope they bring
As we sing about Your light
While this aging world staggers by.

So take the rough and tumble on the chin
Fear not of people and their din
For this life is hope and fear,
The pain rides with the cheer."

Go Back To Your Own Country

I'm a man who was born in England
And I was flabbergasted you see
When this lady jeered with her terrible sneer:
"Go back to your own country!"

I was sitting minding my own business
At the back of the number twenty-three
And this lady glared like a grizzly bear:
"Go back to your own country!"

"I can tell by your bushy joint eyebrows
And your looks foreign and swarthy
That fist-length beard isn't welcomed here
Go back to your own country!!!"

"You swarmed into our nation
We welcomed you in generously
But you brought your whole clan from Pakistan
The ain't a job left in our country."

Well I'm sure that you can appreciate
I was furious as wolverine
"You cheeky sort!" Began my retort,
"I was born in this country!!!"

"I possess a British passport
I pay my taxes and VAT
What cheek you've got! And I'll tell you what
I've had enough of this country!"

So instead of heading on to my business
To the airport I went angrily
Off to join my dad in Islamabad
Going back to my own country.

When I landed and retained my baggage
Strolled out into Rawalpindi
I became cornered by some crafty beggars
The vagabonds of my own country:

"Have mercy my dear brother,
Give us all a thousand rupees,"
"Do I look like a jerk?" I said with a smirk,
"You're a shame on your own country!"

Then they stared at me with astonishment
saying: "listen you posh Englandee!
Don't you lecture us with your gora accent
Go back to your own country!"

They left with some huffing and puffing
And I stood there dejectedly
Feeling quite injured by their withering words
Do I belong to any country?

Then my dad appeared at Arrivals
And we left in those dinky taxis
Said some prayers and praise at my Dada's grave
But I slept that night with great unease.

When I woke it was like a lush garden
People smiled and greeted me
Spirits dressed in light and charming sprites
"Welcome back to your own country!"

Then I recognized my Dada Abba
With a face young and serene
"listen here my boy," he announced with joy,
"Paradise is your true country!"

"The earth is the world of the traveller
you don't belong there you see
So until it's time to leave your body behind
You have to bear with adversities."

"Your spirit will never be contented
With the earth and the seven seas
The truth is clear, you don't belong there
Timeless is your true country."

"So while you're alive and kicking
Don't stress about some mockery
To reach the bliss of a houri's kiss
Bear with ignorance patiently."

"In this world you're always an outsider
You're like a wandering refugee
Your ego and pride fight the spirit inside
They don't live in your true country."

"Don't yearn for a country or nation
Live with courage and harmony
Don't be perturbed by some ignorant words
In time you'll reach your true country."

With this wonderful dream in my memory
I returned to my country of residency
My old routine, the number twenty-three,
There sat the woman who had abused me.

When the bus stopped I saw her struggling
with her bags and her property.
I repressed my rage and offered her some aid
She smiled and accepted me.

"Thank you for your help," said the woman,
"I'm very impressed you see,
But at the end of the day, I just have to say
GO BACK TO YOUR OWN COUNTRY!!!"

Notes:
Dada Abba: phrase for paternal grandfather in Urdu
Houri: maiden in paradise
Englandee: nickname in Pakistan for British Pakistani

The Rise of Strump and Baghdadi

A New Yorker called Ronald Strump
With Latinos and Muslims, he had the hump!
For him all the Latinos were a bunch of druggies
And Muslims were a national security worry.

He'd flick his quiff and pick and sniff
While screaming firebrand speeches
The Muslims angered him so much
He'd go all pink like peaches!

"Don't let an Arab in your house!
Don't trust your local Muslim!
If we dignify their faith
They'll burkafy our women!
They'll build their mosques in our kiosks
They'll drown us in Sharia
They'll turn Broadway and Hollywood
Into replicas of Mecca!
If you make me President
I'll neutralise the roaches!
I'll exorcise these sand demons!
I'll send them packing onto coaches!"

Spitting a rant in the Levant
Shook a gangster called Baghdadi

"The infidels will roast in Hell!"
He roared at his jihadis.
"We'll kill them all, they'll swoon and fall
Like subjects clutching our feet
We'll take their wives as concubines
And make their men burn pig-meat!
And as for all those hypocrites
Who dare to call themselves Muslims
If they don't offer me their pledge
I'll cut off from them two limbs!"

The people flogged these demagogues
With public condemnation
"They're so dumb, these Nazi-scum
They're both abominations!"
The vast majority felt safe
And laughed at Strump and Baghdadi
These two men were rather thick
They'd turn into nobody.

But Ronald Strump, who had the hump
And the plunderer Baghdadi
Still called each other's worlds a dump
Still marched along, foolhardy.

And so bemused were the multitude
By the rise of Strump and Baghdadi

They stood dismayed one fateful day

When outside stood Strump and Baghdadi

Behind them flanked in rows and ranks

Their foot-soldiers all ready

"It's World War Three!" Cried Strump with glee

Baghdadi yelled: "I'm the Mahdi!"

And as the bombs and knives and guns

Went crazy on the home streets

So bemused were the multitude

By the rise of Strump and Baghdadi.

The March of the Gazan Babies

While the rank and file of defiant Hamas
Locked down the city for imminent attack
While the suffering mothers of the Gaza strip
Gathered up their brood for a perilous trip
While the tanks and the trucks of the IDF
Charged along the highway like a crazed express
While the world looked on, angered and dismayed
On their glowing screens, many miles away,
A rousing crack and a jolting thud
Left palpitations in the Gazan mud
Then the street lights shattered
And the shop fronts rattled
From the Daraj Quarter to Sabra and Daraj
The Gazans feared for the wrath of God
More than the scheming of the vile Likud
Some felt the ground thumping under their feet,
They could sense some marching from Sheikh Radwan street,
"Get ready for war," roared a Hamas guard
"The Yahuud are here, in our own backyard!"
And they snapped and clicked their guns in place
Waiting for the order, grimace on the face,
And the marching grew like a pounding drum
As if approached a hundred thousand,
With rifles ready and their wits aware

The guards stood poised in the dusty air
But a voice yelled out and he dropped in a swoon
"Inna lillahi wa inna ilayhi raajioon!"
Before the eyes of the Gazan squad
A sight befell them, a miracle of God,
Babies wrapped in white, marched along the street
Babies dead before and some only just this week,
Hundreds swamped the scene, charging along
Punching the air, while chanting this song:
"For shame! For shame! Ya Bani Israeel!
Our great grandfather Abraham
Disowns your butchery!
For shame! For shame! Ya Bani Israeel!
You dropped your bombs in the clear night sky
And killed us in our sleep!
For shame! For shame! Ya Bani Israeel!
We were hungry birds in a threadbare nest
Meagre scraps for a meal!
For shame! For shame! Ya Bani Israeel!
We were just little vessels, thirsty for life
And you drowned us in your steel!
For shame! For shame! Ya Bani Israeel!
How will you face the Lord of the Worlds?
On the day that all's revealed!
For shame! For shame! Ya Umma! Muslimeen!

You swim in your oil, make others toil
Standing by while our wounds bleed!
For shame! For shame! Ya Umma! Muslimeen!
You love this world, which is just absurd,
It's just a passing dream!
For shame! For shame! Ya Umma! Muslimeen!
When will you rise from your laziness?
For this life is fantasy!
For shame! For shame! Our fellow human-beings!
We killed in our nappies, not a crime to our names
And you just sat by and disagreed.
For shame! For shame! Our fellow human beings!
If you don't act soon, another wave of children
Will just be some figures for history."

Where Did You Go Last Night?

He arose with gleaming eyes and the traces of last night
still smouldering from the ardour of the tryst.
From her side of the bed, she sat up, carefully observing
Pangs of suspicion swelling, sensing some foreboding:

"Where did you go last night? Why came you home so late?"
Then like a hawk she scanned for clues upon his face.
But he just sighed so sweetly and smiled forever.
"Well?" She replied, her fears making her shiver.
He said: "after all this time I finally met Her."
"Her!" she cried, "I should have known better!"
And then her hands fixed round his neck like a pair of fetters.
"Who is she? What's the name of this strumpet!?"
Just audible he gasped: "some call Her Layla, but She's not a harlot."
She dug her nails deeper into his neck:
"How many nights this floozy have you met?!"
He winced and said: "last night was our first meeting."
"And this morning I will inflict upon you an almighty beating!"
Shaking him like a rag doll she screamed: "what is she like?"
He coughed out: "none can compare to Her delights."
Enraged, she roared: "where does this minx live?!"
"You'll never find Her with your five senses."
She sat, head in her hands, broken and tearful:

"Why did you this to me for I was ever faithful?!"

And sobbing like a wretch she dashed into the street.

He just sat there, feeling the winds of love so sweet.

But though the Beloved One had brought him so near,

As the hours passed he began to fear

For his wife, because deep down he really did love her

She was his trusted friend, his partner, his succour.

The night closed in, his heart filled with regret:

"My love for You has chased away my dear pet!"

And through the night he couldn't taste any sleep

He was overcome with worry and raw grief.

Then as the dawn broke clear and light shone far and wide

She appeared in the doorway, with the deepest, piercing eyes.

He started up: "where did you go last night? Where in heaven!?"

To his joy, she said: "well, you see, I finally met Him!"

Notes:

In Sufism, Islamic spirituality, spiritual aspirants sometimes address the Divine Presence using the feminine pronouns in their attempt to describe the beauty of the presence that has entered their hearts. Thus, in Sufi poetry, it is common for Sufi poets to address Allah Most High with epithets like Layla, Salma, Ainee, Lubna and others. In the above poem, the wife's initial misunderstanding of her husband's revelation comes full circle, as she herself experiences the Divine, to her husband's surprise.

Here I am exploring the time-worn concept of divine love through the prism of marital relationships.

If The Man On The Moon Were A Mozlem

By Robert Warrenjehad Denser and Anna Arabaiter Cooltar

If the man on the moon were a Mozlem!
Why, I sure wouldn't be so surprised.
Coz everywhere you step in our nation
There be mosques and their holy cries!

We let them into our blessed borders,
Gave em chances that they never woulda got.
Coz they come from the land of the A Rabs!
From their sultanic satanic despots!

And what kind thanx do they give uz?
For giving them hope and glory?
Instead of handshakes or assimilate
We get mosques, halal shops and curry!

So if the man on the moon were a Mozlem!
Why, you can bet on what he gonna do,
He gonna fill up all those holes and craters
And build a mega-mosque the size of Peru!

Now it's time for some noise from all you patriots!

We gotta stand against this Mozlem threat!
If we don't do it now you'll regret it
Coz Obama'll let em build a Caliphate!

Don't be taken in by those gutless apologists!
And all the bull that they have to declare!
Like them tell you that the Mozlems are citizens
And uz patriots are mongerers of scare!

They tell you just take a look at our doctors
And some of the engineers that we got
They be Mozlems, so don't tar the majority,
Don't tarnish the whole damn lot!

What the hell have these Mozlems done for uz?
Save from terror and their Islamo-fascist laws?
Now we gotta be treated by their darn doctors,
With their bogus cures from land of the moors!

Now don't you dare call us a bunch of bigots!
Juz because we don't like Izlaam
We got perfect right to express our opinions
And gobble up a juicy piece of ham!

So if the man on the moon were a Mozlem!

Why I'd go and give him a piece of my mind!
For invading a land that he don't belong to!
Which without him was doing just fine!

Listen here, patriots, to our message!
Be aware of their terrible ideas...
No you don't need to read any books yourself
Or speak to Muzlims screeching down your ears!

All you need is our informative website
We did the research on Sharia and Muftis
We didn't need to talk to any experts
Just the homepage of Anwar Awlaki!

If the man on the moon was a Mozlem,
This is just what I'd say
"Get your ass down you don't belong there chum!
Coz the moon belongs to the U S of A!!"

Notes:
This poem is a satire on US Islamophobes, Robert Spencer and Ann Coulter.

You Can't Judge A Bloke By Appearance

I'll never forget, when my ears were still wet,
And I learned one of life's painful lessons.
I won't be surprised if you've learned this yourself
You can't judge a bloke by appearance.

It was when I was ten, when the days didn't end,
I was having a really bad hair day.
My fringe: quite misshapen, my sideburns: forsaken,
So mum said: "Get a haircut and hairspray!"

I entered soon after, the Italian barbers
Whose hair was considerably wavy.
He gave me a wink, and a curious blink
By habit; he was a little bit crazy.

I sat with a gig, by a bloke with a wig
Just sitting there, minding my business.
When I glanced straight ahead at the barber's mirror
The sight that I saw left me speechless.

He sat there, a giant, an abominable tyrant,
With a scar on his face which made him look fiery.
His skin was as tough as the mail of a titan
And to top it off, he was glaring right at me!

I panicked, dismayed, looking the other way,
This bloke sent me in a fit of tight shivers.
He looked like a butcher, or a serial killer
And I'm sure that he wanted my liver.

Perhaps he would rob us, right after his haircut
Tie us up and never release us.
He'd break us in two, feed us to his wolves
I was trapped by this human tyrannosaurus.
The terror entwined in my innocent mind,
When suddenly I came to my senses,
The barber had finished his last ever haircut
And above me towered my nemesis.

I was stuck to my chair by his punishing stare
As he stood arching over the barber
He reached in his pocket; my heart was a rocket,
Any minute he'd brandish a chain-saw!

I gripped onto my seat, accepting defeat,
Despairing, I was too young for mass murders.
When the barber just stood there and looked at this man-
bear and said:
"Are you up for some snooker?"
I thought that was queer, questioning my ears,

Has our barber turned totally barmy?
This man for his humour would torture a panda,
He replied: "Yeh I'll play; then we'll order a curry!"

My heart went berserk, like a surge of fireworks,
I realised he wasn't a murderous zombie!
Not a man from the mountains or chainsaw wielder
He was one of the barber's old cronies!

This man paid and left, giving me no eye contact,
And I just sat there feeling terribly stupid.
I misjudged his appearance out of sheer prejudice
And from then on, my world seemed to broaden.

So I tell you in case, you see a strange face,
Which fills you with fear and suspicions
Just remember my tale, which ended in shame
You just can't judge a bloke by appearance!

The Homecoming Of My Old Friend

One day, a painful memory shook my heart,
My old friend had served me since my birth,
And I had cast him out onto the street,
Denying his undying faithfulness.
For my old friend was becoming wearisome,
Especially now I'd made new, trendy friends,
In these progressing times he seemed passé,
My friends would snigger at my companion.
So, I barged him out onto the lonely street
I slammed the door as he began reasoning,
I convinced myself he was an inconvenience,
I assured my friends I had forsaken him.
Many days and weeks passed gradually,
I felt the world vibrating at my feet,
His knocking had halted some time ago,
But still I knew he lingered there, outside.
So I threw off all my guilt and held my breath,
Then leapt into the mires of my desires.
I plunged in hordes of feigned relationships,
I hosted great, extravagant soirees,
Fleeting ecstasies were my preoccupations,
My house bulged with gate-crashers gushing in,
My heart sagged with intruders surging in.
Until one day, as I jigged around my room,

Encircled by my artificial friends,
They closed in on me, stifling my breast,
They pressured me to offer them my heart,
When a slow knock rocked against my door
Its reverberation left a thunderous roar,
My body trembled like a shaken leaf
From deep within arose familiarity,
I staggered to and fro, shielding my ears,
But still the knocks resounded, thundering.
And then the realisation struck me down,
My abandoned friend was waiting in the cold.
And as this certainty aroused my heart,
Tears of shame ran, searing my desires,
Each drop fell, and my heart was up in flames,
The intruders fled, shrieking in agony.
I moved towards the knocking on my door
The tense smiles of my friends stood in the way,
Attempting to divert my attention,
They promised untold pleasure if I stayed,
But when they realised I was intent
They grabbed my legs and fought to drag me back
Their wailed and cried revealing their dismay,
And I just kicked them off with bitterness.
And so I stood there, facing my front door
I turned and saw my friends gaping in horror,

I turned the handle with my quivering hand
My heart lamented as the door opened,
I dreaded facing him after so long,
I planned I'd throw myself before his feet,
When suddenly every single thing vanished
My house, my friends, myself and nothing else remained.
And then I found myself not in my room
But on the lonely street, there, shivering
Before me stood a great, glistening door
It opened and my old friend emerged,
He covered me with warm, comforting robes
He wrapped me in His unifying glow,
He sheltered me from sorrow and the cold,
And I had been a homeless, wretched soul,
And by His love I'd finally returned home.

ABOUT THE AUTHOR

Novid Shaid is an English teacher from the UK, who has taught in various secondary schools for over fifteen years. His first published work is the mystical thriller novel: *The Hidden Ones*, which is available on Amazon.

He also shares short stories and poems on his website, www.novid.co.uk, and has written a play called *The War, the Lift and the Separatists*. His next novel is an allegorical tale called:
The Journey Overboard.

29303205R00086

Printed in Great Britain
by Amazon